Scholastic's

HALL OF FAME

by Katherine Noll
and Tracey West

SCHOLASTIC INC.

New York   Toronto   London   Auckland   Sydney
Mexico City   New Delhi   Hong Kong   Buenos Aires

ISBN 0-439-68674-1

12 11 10 9 8 7 6 5 4   5 6 7 8 9/0

Printed in the U.S.A.
First printing, October 2004

HANGIN' in the HALL of FAME

There are hundreds of Pokémon in the universe, and trainers are discovering new Pokémon all the time. Each Pokémon is special in its own way. But it takes a really special Pokémon to make it into our Pokémon Hall of Fame.

Check out the stats in this book to find out which Pokémon is the biggest; which is hard to capture; which Pokémon seem to be loved by fans, and more. See if your favorite Pokémon made our list!

And that's not all. In this Hall of Fame you'll also learn about the powerful attacks, the challenging trainers, and even the funny moments from the TV show. We've made sure to include the whole world of Pokémon, so there's something for everyone.

So what are you waiting for? Put on your cap, and get ready to tour our Pokémon Hall of Fame. By the time you're done, you'll be a real Pokémon expert. Who knows? You just might earn a place in the Hall of Fame yourself — as the world's greatest Pokémon fan!

COUNTING TO TEN

If you're a typical Pokémon trainer, then you've probably got a few top ten lists in your head already. You know your top ten Pokémon to use in battle or your top ten all-around favorite Pokémon. If you're like most trainers, then the list keeps changing the more you train and capture new Pokémon.

This section is full of our top ten picks
in different categories: ten great Pokémon, ten fabulous *new* Pokémon, ten
greatest battles, bad guys, and other
greats.

Of course, the world of Pokémon is
always changing. Bigger, better, and
faster Pokémon are being discovered every day. Smarter
and meaner bad guys will be
challenging Ash and his friends.
So enjoy these lists while they
last. Who knows what surprises the
future will bring?

TEN GREAT POKéMON

Scholastic's pick

What's so great about these ten Pokémon? They've all got awesome attacks, lots of power, and are super hard to beat. Any Pokémon trainer would be lucky to have these fabulous fighters in his or her arsenal!

BLAZIKEN™

Looking at a cute Torchic, you might never guess that it evolves into this fierce Pokémon. A combination of Fire and Fighting elements make for a red-hot mix of power.

CELEBI™

This sweet-looking Pokémon has one of the most incredible powers in the Pokémon world: the ability to travel through time.

CHARIZARD™

It looks like a giant lizard and fights like a champion. Not many Pokémon can resist its scorching Fire attacks.

LATIAS™

Like her male counterpart, Latios, this Dragon/Psychic Pokémon is very intelligent and can understand human speech.

7

LATIOS™

This unusual Pokémon can fly faster than a jet plane! He also has the ability to project images from his mind into the minds of his opponents.

LUGIA™

This legendary Pokémon's psychic powers are so strong that it must live at the bottom of the ocean. Lugia can "speak" to humans by projecting words into their mind.

MEW™

One of the most difficult Pokémon to capture, Mew is rarely seen. It stayed hidden for centuries until it emerged to protect the world from its clone, Mewtwo.

MEWTWO™

Scientists cloned Mew, hoping they could control the powerful Pokémon. They were wrong. Mewtwo is almost impossible to catch—and even harder to control.

PIKACHU™

It's a rare Pokémon that packs a double punch of power and personality. Not only are Pikachu's Electric attacks ultraeffective, but it's cute and loyal besides. Who could ask for a better Pokémon?

RAYQUAZA™

This sinister-looking Dragon/Flying Pokémon stands 23 feet tall and has been known to terrorize cities with its extreme attacks. To catch it, you'll need plenty of Ultra Balls—not to mention plenty of patience!

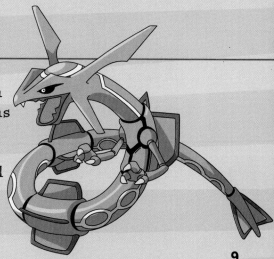

9

TEN BRAND-NEW* POKéMON

Scholastic's pick

*from Ruby and Sapphire Pokémon Advance

ABSOL™

If you catch sight of this Dark Pokémon, run for cover! Every time Absol is spotted, a natural disaster like an earthquake or tidal wave hits.

GROUDON™

According to ancient myth, the world's continents were formed when massive Groudon roamed the earth.

JIRACHI™

This mysterious Pokémon is said to sleep for a thousand years. It will awaken if you sing to it in a pure voice—and then it will grant your wishes!

KYOGRE™

If you see Kyogre, better get out your umbrella! This Water Pokémon can create storm clouds that make rain.

MUDKIP™

The fin on top of Mudkip's head may look unusual, but it's very useful. Because the fin can sense movements in the air and water around it, Mudkip can navigate without opening its eyes!

SALAMENCE™

How did Salamance get its wings? The story goes that this Dragon Pokémon so desperately wanted to fly that a mutation formed and wings sprouted from its back. Salamence's dream came true!

SCEPTILE™

This Grass Pokémon's tail is covered with super sharp leaves. It's also very agile and travels through the forest by leaping from tree to tree.

SWAMPERT™

The final evolved form of Mudkip, super strong Swampert can drag a one-ton boulder with ease. Its sharp eyesight allows it to see when swimming in murky water.

TORCHIC™

Aw, isn't Torchic cute? Not if you're battling one. This little Pokémon breathes scorching flames that reach 1,800 degrees Fahrenheit!

TREECKO™

If you look closely at Treecko's feet, you'll see small hooks that enable this Grass Pokémon to scale vertical walls. Its thick tail is useful for thumping opponents during a battle.

TEN GREATEST BAD GUYS OF ALL TIME

Scholastic's pick

ANNIE™

In *Pokémon Heroes*, mean teen Annie and her partner Oakley of Team Rocket are out to steal a rare jewel — even if it means capturing an innocent Latias in the process!

BUTLER™

In the movie *Jirachi: Wish Maker*, Ash and his friends meet a friendly magician. But he's really a Team Magma scientist intent on capturing Jirachi for his own selfish means.

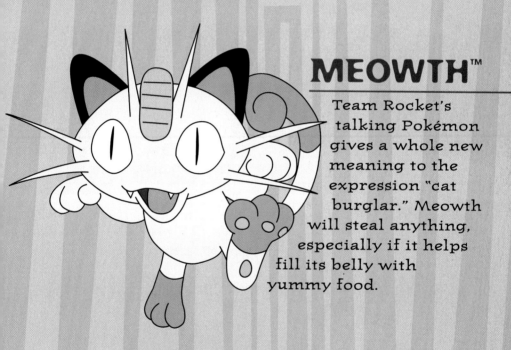

MEOWTH™

Team Rocket's talking Pokémon gives a whole new meaning to the expression "cat burglar." Meowth will steal anything, especially if it helps fill its belly with yummy food.

GIOVANNI™

He may stay in the shadows, stroking his Persian, but Giovanni is the leader and mastermind of Team Rocket. His agents are trained to steal money, treasures, and of course, rare Pokémon—and bring them back to the Boss.

LAWRENCE III™

He's a wealthy Pokémon collector who would rather cage his Pokémon than train them. In *Pokémon the Movie 2000*, his attempts to capture the legendary birds Zapdos, Moltres, and Articuno nearly destroy the world!

JESSIE™

Jessie may be smarter than her partner, James, but her hot temper gets her into trouble every time. She and James and Meowth almost always mess things up, but not before they make things very difficult for Ash and his friends!

IRON MASK MARAUDER™

One of Team Rocket's top executives, Iron Mask is known for capturing Pokémon using a Dark Ball, which taints them with evil and increases their powers to the highest level. In *Pokémon 4Ever*, Iron Mask uses a Dark Ball on an innocent Celebi!

JAMES™

James used to be a poor little rich boy, but he left all that behind to live a life of crime for Team Rocket. Along with Jessie and Meowth, his main goal is to capture Ash's Pikachu. But they haven't succeeded yet!

BUTCH™ AND CASSIDY™

This team of Team Rocket agents is a favorite of Giovanni's. They're meaner and smarter than their counterparts, Jessie and James. Fortunately for Ash, they're not much better at stealing Pikachu!

OAKLEY™

Although Oakley and her partner, Annie, are only teenagers, they have already become master thieves. Jessie and James could probably learn a thing or two from their fellow Team Rocket agents!

TEN GREATEST BATTLES OF ALL TIME

Scholastic's pick

PIKACHU™ vs. SPEAROW™

Season 1, Episode 101: I Choose You!

When Ash got Pikachu, his very first Pokémon, from Professor Oak, Pikachu didn't obey Ash at all. Ash was sure his first Pokémon journey was going to be a disaster— and it almost was, when a flock of angry Spearow attacked. Ash put himself in peril to save Pikachu, and Pikachu returned the favor by using the last of its power to fight off the Spearow. Ash and Pikachu formed a bond during that battle that hasn't been broken yet!

ASH™ vs. HARRISON™

Season 6, Episode 609: Play With Fire! and Episode 610: Johto Photo Finish

After traveling all over the Johto Region, Ash decided to compete in the ultimate contest there: the Johto League Silver Conference. He defeated his longtime rival, Gary, and then went on to face Harrison, a trainer from the Hoenn Region. After a long, difficult, and strategic battle, there were two Pokémon left standing: Ash's Charizard and Harrison's Blaziken. Both Pokémon battled fiercely, but in the end, Charizard fainted— and Ash headed off on his next adventure.

ASH™ vs. BRAWLEY™— THE REMATCH

Season 6, Episode 643: Just One of the Geysers

When Ash got to Dewford Town, he headed right to the gym and challenged Brawley, the gym leader. Brawley used his Fighting Pokémon Machop and Makuhita along with a lot of fighting spirit to defeat Ash. But Ash didn't give up. He trained really hard for the rematch. The second time he beat Brawley— and earned his badge.

ASH™ vs. RITCHIE™

Season 2, Episode 226: Friend and Foe Alike!

Losing a big battle to another trainer is tough, but losing one to a friend is even tougher. When Ash competed in the Indigo League, he made friends with a trainer named Ritchie. In the fifth round of the tournament, Ash and Ritchie had to battle each other! Ritchie defeated Ash with a Pikachu named Sparky, and it hit Ash hard. But he and Ritchie remained friends.

CHARIZARD™ vs. POLIWRATH™

Season 2, Episode 252: Charizard Chills

Ash's Charizard used to have an attitude problem. It evolved early and was convinced it could beat any opponent without Ash's help. Then a trainer came along with a Poliwrath that Charizard couldn't beat. Charizard finally learned to obey Ash—and the two of them got along much better from then on.

ASH'S™ POKéMON vs. ANTHONY'S PELIPPER™

Season 6, Episode 622: You Said a Mouthful

While traveling in the Hoenn Region, Ash came across an unofficial gym led by a trainer named Anthony. Anthony battled Ash using Pelipper, a Water Bird Pokémon with Water and Flying attacks. So how on earth did Pelipper use Vine Whip against Ash's Treecko, Flame Thrower against Taillow, and Thunder Attack against Pikachu? Because Anthony was hiding Poké Balls inside Pelipper's large beak—and secretly calling on other Pokémon during the battle!

ASH™ vs. MISTY™: THE TOTODILE DUEL

Season 3, Episode 346: The Totodile Duel

When Ash and Misty saw a cute Totodile playing in the water, they both threw Lure Balls at it—but neither one was sure who caught it. They battled to see who would get to keep Totodile.

Togepi battled Pikachu, Chikorita battled Staryu, and in the end, Bulbasaur battled Poliwhirl to lead Ash to victory.

ASH™ vs. MISTY™: THE WHIRL CUP

Season 5, Episode 508: The Perfect Match!

While traveling around the Whirl Islands, both Ash and Misty decided to compete in the Whirl Cup competition. They ended up facing each other in one of the final rounds. In a surprise move, Misty's Psyduck came out of its Poké Ball accidentally and defeated Ash's Kingler! Ash lost, and Misty moved on to the last round.

CYNDAQUIL™ vs. SKARMORY™

Season 3, Episode 347: Hot Matches!

Ash's Cyndaquil should have had no trouble beating Skarmory. After all, Cyndaquil is a Fire Pokémon, and Skarmory is weak against Fire attacks. But Ash and his Cyndaquil learned a lesson when a female trainer's Skarmory stood up to Cyndaquil in a fierce battle.

PIKACHU™ vs. TAILLOW™

Season 6, Episode 616: You Can Never Taillow

Ash and Pikachu were walk-ing alone in Petalburg Forest when they came across a flock of wild Taillow. Ash decided to capture one of the Taillow, and the agile Flying Pokémon fought with Pikachu. Taillow refused to give in to Pikachu's Electric attacks—but Ash caught it in the end.

WHO'S THAT POKéMON?
(part 1)

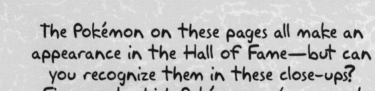

The Pokémon on these pages all make an
appearance in the Hall of Fame—but can
you recognize them in these close-ups?
Figure out which Pokémon we've zoomed
in on and write the name in the space
below each picture.

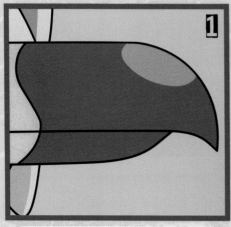

wingul

me??????

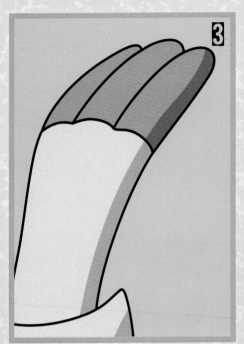

3

4

Peliperies

Blasickin

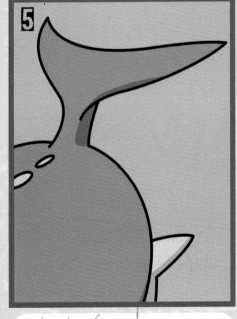

5

6

Wialod

Tailow

Belleson

Sunktann

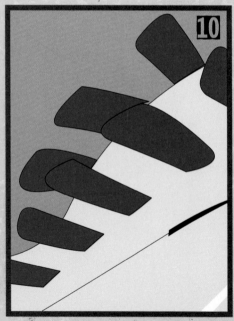

OH-HO

UUILA

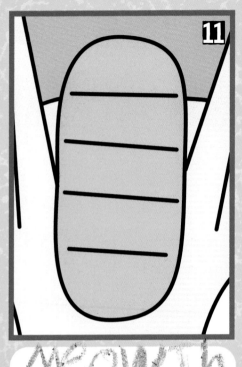

11

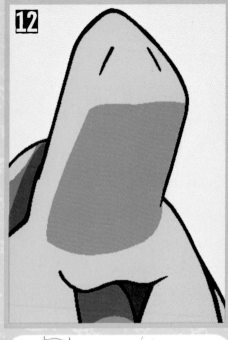

12

meowth

Phanify

13

14

Entei

Sleykdig

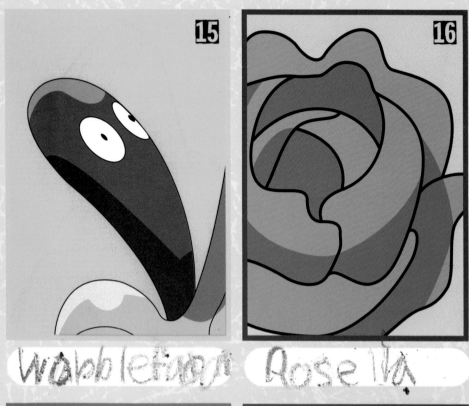

15 | 16

wobbletoon | Rose lla

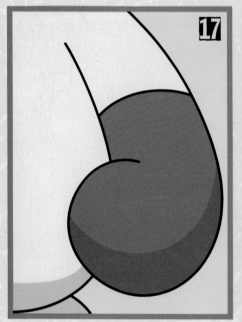

17 | 18

todidiel

19

Mewtwo

20

Hanten

21

Slowpoké

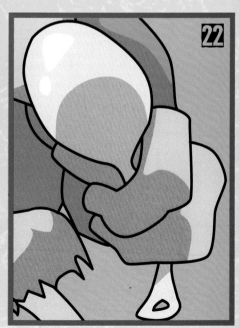

22

Alicsur

29

23. Unhown

24. ~~Gardu~~

25. PSduch

26. Archikoono

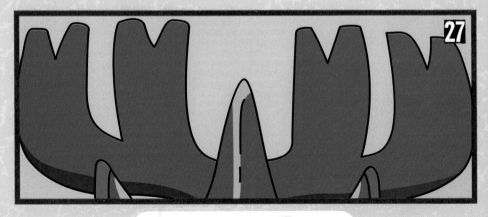

27. ~~Rutorp~~

30

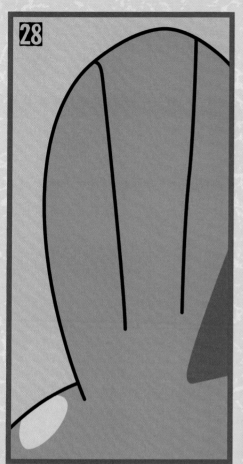

28

29

theeko

30

Mudkip

Jiglypuf

31

B.

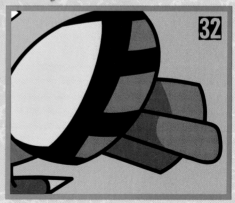

32

Nate

33

Pikachu

34

Serperior

35

woolflobot

37

swampert

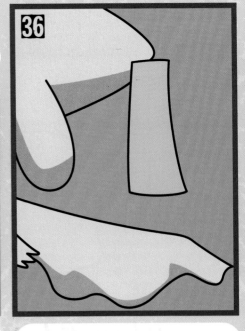

36

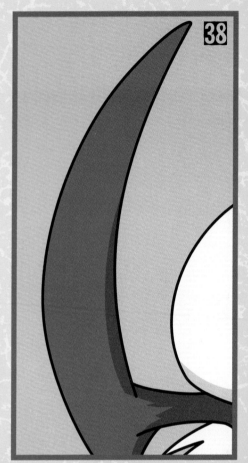

38

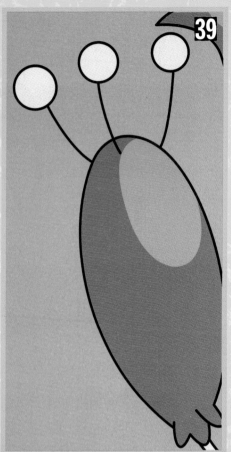

39

Absole

Skitty

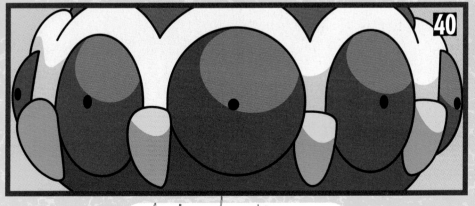

40

kladol

EXTREME POKéMON

Each Pokémon is special in its own way. Some are fast, some are slow. Some are big, some are small. Some are sweet, and some are scary.

In every category, though, one or two Pokémon stand out from the crowd. In this section, we'll be taking a look at the Pokémon at the top of their class. These Pokémon make you turn

your head when you see them walking--
or slithering, or flying, or exploding--
down the street.

    See if any of your Pokémon are
big enough, bad enough, or stand
out enough to make the list. If not,
maybe you'd better get out there
and catch some! No trainer's
stable of Pokémon would be
complete without these special
guys.

FUNNY POKéMON

Squirtle™ and Totodile™

What is it about Ash's Water Pokémon? They've got lots of personality, that's for sure. Their antics have earned Squirtle and Totodile the title of Funniest Pokémon. Maybe it's something in the water!

Squirtle™

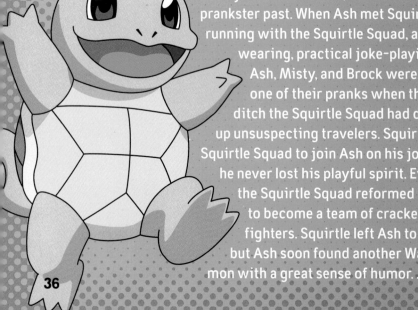

Squirtle may look like every other cute and cuddly Water Pokémon, but Ash's Squirtle has a prankster past. When Ash met Squirtle, it was running with the Squirtle Squad, a sunglass-wearing, practical joke-playing gang. Ash, Misty, and Brock were victims of one of their pranks when they fell into a ditch the Squirtle Squad had dug to trip up unsuspecting travelers. Squirtle left the Squirtle Squad to join Ash on his journey, but he never lost his playful spirit. Eventually, the Squirtle Squad reformed their ways to become a team of crackerjack fire-fighters. Squirtle left Ash to rejoin them, but Ash soon found another Water Poké-mon with a great sense of humor. . . .

Totodile™

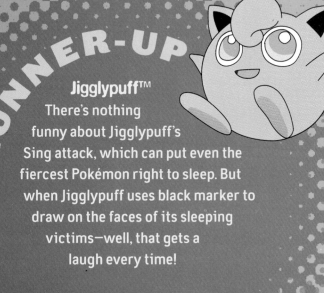

If Squirtle is a prankster, then Totodile is a show-off. When Ash first saw Totodile, it was doing a silly dance in the middle of a river. Ash and Misty both wanted Totodile so badly that they battled each other for it! Ash won, and Totodile has been entertaining Ash ever since by performing tricks in the water—like juggling Magikarp! Ash can always turn to Totodile for a laugh. Of course, Totodile is tough in battle, too. When Ash calls Totodile into action, you can be sure his opponents aren't smiling.

RUNNER-UP

Jigglypuff™

There's nothing funny about Jigglypuff's Sing attack, which can put even the fiercest Pokémon right to sleep. But when Jigglypuff uses black marker to draw on the faces of its sleeping victims—well, that gets a laugh every time!

37

BIG POKéMON

Wailord™

It's hard to believe that this huge Pokémon fits in a tiny Poké Ball! Of course, to get it inside a Poké Ball you have to catch it first—if you can. At more than 47 feet long, this Water Pokémon is the longest Pokémon by far. It also weighs a whopping 878 pounds.

Wailord, of course, is the evolved form of Wailmer. The average height of this cute Ball Whale Pokémon is 6 feet, 7 inches. That means that Wailmer gets more than seven times bigger when it evolves! Now that's evolution.

RUNNERS-UP

ONYX™	RAYQUAZA™	GYARADOS™
28 feet, 10 inches	23 feet	21 feet, 4 inches

SMALL POKéMON

Sunkern™

If you're not careful, you might miss seeing this Pokémon altogether. After all, it's only one inch tall!

Sunkern is tiny, all right, but it still has an impressive array of attacks, including Mega Drain, Sunny Day, Synthesis, and Giga Drain. If a Sunkern gets a lot of experience using those attacks, it will evolve into a happy-faced Sunflora, which stands more than two feet tall. So each little Sunkern has something to look forward to.

RUNNERS-UP

These two Pokémon are both only eight inches tall:

DIGLETT™ The hole-digging Ground Pokémon.

NATU™ The mysterious Psychic/Flying Pokémon.

LIGHT POKéMON

Gastly™ and Haunter™

It makes sense that these two Pokémon are the lightest around—they are Ghost Pokémon, after all. In fact, Gastly is made up entirely of gas. That's why Gastly and its evolved form, Haunter, weigh only one-fifth of a pound each.

Both of these Pokémon prove that you don't have to weigh much to be tough. Besides being Ghost Pokémon, they're also Poison Pokémon, and that's a tough combination to beat. So if you're a weakling who gets picked on by bigger Pokémon trainers, don't despair. Just look to light-as-air Gastly and Haunter for inspiration!

REMEMBER WHEN...

Ash, Misty, and Brock were traveling through a spooky forest, and they began to see illusions, like scary faces in the trees and glowing balls of light. It took a Hoothoot to show them the cause of the illusions: a forest full of Haunter and its evolved form, Gengar!

HEAVY POKéMON

Groudon™

Massive Groudon weighs a whopping 2,095 pounds—the only Pokémon to weigh more than a ton. Legend says that an ancient battle occurred between Groudon and Kyogre. Groudon lost and has been in a deep sleep for years.

In the movie *Jirachi: Wish Maker*, a member of Team Magma tries to revive Groudon and ends up creating a monstrous, mutated version of the Pokémon.

RUNNER-UP

Metagross™ The next heaviest Pokémon, Metagross, weighs 1,213 pounds, about half as much as Groudon. Metagross is heavy because it's made of solid steel. It also has the distinction of having an unusual element combination: Metagross and its preevolutions are all Steel/Psychic Pokémon.

SLOW POKéMON

Slowpoke™

Snorlax is lazy, but it will move . . . especially if there is food to be found. But Slowpoke hates to move at all! Sometimes it's hard to tell the difference between a Slowpoke and a statue.

How slow is Slowpoke? If it is attacked, it takes a full five seconds before it even realizes it is in pain. And to evolve, all it has to do is stick its long tail in the ocean. If a Shellder clamps onto its tail, Slowpoke becomes a Slowbro, just like that!

Now *that's* lazy.

SMART POKéMON

Alakazam™

You may think your Pokémon are smart, but with Alakazam, the proof is in the numbers. This Psychic Pokémon has an IQ of 5,000. That makes it smarter than the world's most powerful supercomputers!

Of course, Alakazam's super brain is no use if it gets stuck with a trainer without any smarts. If you're lucky enough to get an Alakazam, use it wisely—and watch it decimate your opponents!

DUMB POKéMON

Slowpoke™

Poor Slowpoke! Not only is its body slow, its brain is pretty slow, too. This Pokémon is no genius, but with attacks like Water Gun, Amnesia, and Psychic, it can get the job done as well as any Alakazam. It's all in how you train it!

CONFUSED POKéMON

Misty's Psyduck™

Psyduck is a Water Pokémon with an unusual brain. When it gets a headache, it lets loose a torrent of mental energy that can confuse any opponent. But most of the time, Psyduck is the one that is confused! It is always bumping into things or getting lost. And when Misty tries to call on a Pokémon during battle, sometimes Psyduck comes out by mistake! Most of the time Misty is annoyed with her Psyduck, but when the chips are down, Psyduck always pulls through.

Most Psyduck are just as clumsy as Misty's—but there is hope. With enough experience, Psyduck will evolve into the elegant and graceful Golduck. Now that's something to look forward to!

RUNNER-UP

Jessie's Wobbuffet™ At a Pokémon swap meet, Jessie lost her super strong Lickitung—and got a Wobbuffet in exchange. Just like Psyduck, Wobbuffet was always getting lost and coming out of its Poké Ball when it wasn't wanted. Some people think that's exactly the kind of Pokémon Jessie deserves!

MYSTERIOUS POKéMON

Unown™

Unown is a Psychic Pokémon, but it doesn't look much like other Pokémon at all. Unown has a flat, thin body that can usually be found stuck to a wall if it's not swirling around in the air with other Unown. This strange Pokémon can take 26 different forms, each one resembling a letter of the English alphabet.

Unown's power is hidden, but we do know something about it. A professor named Spencer Hale uncovered proof of the Unown, which had been lost ages ago. His daughter, Molly, accidentally unleashed the powers of the Unown, and her dreams came to life! Molly's dreams almost destroyed the world—until Ash and his friends came to save the day. As that story shows, it's still not safe to experiment with the powers of this mysterious Pokémon!

RUNNER-UP

Jirachi™ The story of Jirachi is one of Pokémon's strangest legends. Jirachi is said to have the power to grant wishes. There's just one catch: Jirachi sleeps for a thousand years and only wakes for seven days in between each sleep. If Jirachi senses danger, however, it will defend itself without waking up.

45

BEAUTIFUL POKéMON

Bellossom™ and Roselia™

What is it about Grass Pokémon? So many of them are just lovely to look at. Okay, maybe not Gloom. But we think you'll agree that these two Pokémon could win any beauty contest, petals down.

Bellossom™

Gloom might not be anything to look at, but one of its evolved forms, Bellossom, is positively beautiful. With its colorful flowers, rosy cheeks, and petal skirt, Bellossom looks ready to go to the ball. But what guarantees Bellossom a spot in the Hall of Fame is its Petal Dance. When it dances, its petals rub together and make a ringing sound.

Did you see the Bellossom dance in *Pikachu's Rescue Adventure*? If not, then you missed seeing the world's prettiest Pokémon in action. Keep your eyes open next time you're out searching for Pokémon in tropical areas, because that's where Bellossom can usually be found.

Roselia™

Sure, Roselia has three sharp thorns on top of its head, but they don't detract from its beauty. On each Roselia you'll find one perfect red rose and one perfect blue rose in full bloom. What could be prettier?

This Pokémon may look lovely, but it's also a Poison Pokémon boasting an incredible number of attacks. So while your opponent is smelling the roses, you can have your Roselia launch Stun Spore, Giga Drain, Toxic, or Aroma Therapy. Now that's beautiful!

RUNNER-UP

Ninetails™

This Fire Pokémon has soft white fur, a gorgeous face, and nine beautiful tails tipped with orange. But be careful. If you grab one of its tails, Ninetails may put a thousand-year curse on you!

THE LEGENDARY POKéMON

The Hall of Fame wouldn't be complete without mentioning the Legendary Pokémon. What makes these Pokémon special? Well, they're usually one of a kind; they're rarely seen; they're almost impossible to catch; and they possess super special powers. Ash has been lucky enough to encounter all of these legendary Pokémon at some time or other. If you ever see one, consider yourself lucky, too!

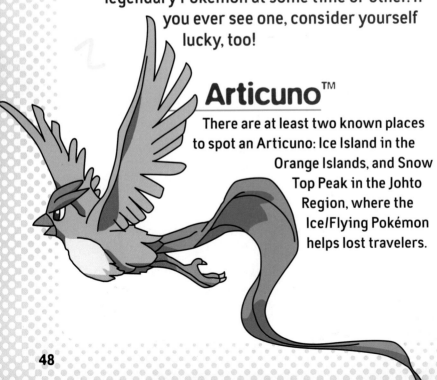

Articuno™

There are at least two known places to spot an Articuno: Ice Island in the Orange Islands, and Snow Top Peak in the Johto Region, where the Ice/Flying Pokémon helps lost travelers.

Moltres™

You can also find Moltres in the Orange Islands, where it lives near fellow legendary birds Articuno, Zapdos, and Lugia. The Fire Pokémon's wings and head constantly glow with burning flames.

Zapdos™

You haven't seen an Electric attack until you've seen Zapdos in action! Some people say you can find Zapdos deep inside the Indigo Plateau Power Plant as well as its home on Lightning Island.

Lugia™

This magnificent Psychic/Flying Pokémon lives deep in the bottom of the ocean. Lugia can communicate with humans by transmitting its thoughts directly to the receiver's mind.

Ho-oh™

The next time you see a rainbow, check the sky around it. There just might be a Ho-oh flying off! This beautiful Fire/Flying Pokémon is said to form rainbows behind it when it soars through the air.

Raikou™

Is that thunder rumbling in the distance? It could be this Electric Pokémon, with a bark that sounds like thunder. It also carries a rain cloud on its back that shoots off powerful thunderbolts!

Entei™

Legend says that a new Entei is born every time a new volcano forms on Earth. The bark of this Fire Pokémon is so powerful that it causes volcanoes to erupt!

Suicune™

This Water Pokémon has a magical ability. It can purify polluted waters by emitting a soft blue healing light. In the movie *Pokémon 4Ever*, Suicune's ability helps save the life of a Celebi.

Celebi™

This adorable Pokémon has one of the most mysterious powers of all the legendary Pokémon: the ability to travel through time. You're most likely to spot this small green Pokémon deep in the forest.

Unown™

This strange Psychic Pokémon appears to have the power to bring dreams to life. That's a power you don't want to mess with!

Mew™

This Psychic Pokémon travels in a protective pink bubble that deflects most opponents' attacks. In fact, most Pokémon experts believe that the only Pokémon that can defeat Mew is its clone, Mewtwo.

Mewtwo™

When scientists created this clone of Mew, they had no idea what the result would be: an incredibly powerful Pokémon that hates its human creators. Mewtwo is the most difficult Pokémon to capture, and Pokémon fans are always arguing about which is stronger: Mew or Mewtwo. In *Mewtwo Strikes Back*, the two battle it out, but Ash stops their battle before either Pokémon is the clear winner.

BEST MASTER OF THE HUMAN LANGUAGE

Team Rocket's Meowth™

Who hasn't heard Team Rocket's signature cry?
"Team Rocket, blast off at the speed of light!" Jessie cries.
"Surrender now, or prepare to fight!" James yells.
"Meowth! That's right!" says Meowth.

What's that? A talking Pokémon? You heard right. Most Pokémon communicate with their trainers by making sounds or speaking their own names over and over. They certainly don't speak English. But Team Rocket's Meowth is different. This clever but misguided Pokémon taught itself to talk to impress a pretty Meowth named Meowsy. It didn't work, but Meowth's power of speech earned it a place with Team Rocket, where it's been causing trouble ever since.

RUNNER-UP

Slowking™ Hidden on Shamouti Island is an ancient temple that holds the secrets to the island's past. And guarding that temple is a majestic Slowking. Unlike its preevolved forms, Slowbro and Slowpoke, this Pokémon is smart—and is one of the few Pokémon to possess the power of speech.

ASH'S
BEST FRIEND

Ash's Pikachu™

Why does Team Rocket keep trying to steal Ash's Pikachu again and again, even though they fail every time? Because they know what most Pokémon fans know: Pikachu is simply the best Pokémon around.

Need proof? Here are just some of the reasons why Ash's Pikachu tops the list of all-time greatest Pokémon.

CUTENESS. Sure, there are plenty of cute Pokémon out there, but with its pointy ears, red cheeks, and cheerful cry of "Pika! Pika!" Pikachu has the cute department all wrapped up.

POWER. Ash has trained Pikachu so well that its Electric attacks are almost impossible to beat. When Ash is in a tight spot in battle, he can always count on Pikachu to shock his opponents!

LOYALTY. Ash has been in plenty of dangerous situations. He's already saved the world more than once! And each time, Pikachu was right by Ash's side. Pikachu will do anything for Ash, even if it means putting itself at risk.

Besides being cute, powerful, and loyal, Pikachu is special in other ways, too. It hates to be inside a Poké Ball and always walks alongside Ash. It has a powerful sense of smell it can use to track and find other Pokémon. There's no question about it: Pikachu is the best of the best!

WHO'S THAT POKéMON?
(part 2)

Can you tell who these Pokémon
Hall of Famers are just by looking
at their outlines? Use the clues to
help you figure out who's who. Then
match the outlines to the stickers
included in this book.

1

Ash catches this
Grass Pokémon
deep in the woods.

treeco

2

May's first
Pokémon.

torchick

3

A cute little
Water Pokémon.

mudkip

4

It's known as the
Disaster Pokémon.

absol

5

This Pokémon saved people who were suffering from droughts.

6

The evolved form of Grovyle.

7

Its attacks include Mud Sport and Muddy Water.

8

It weighs over 2,000 pounds.

One of Ash's
best Pokémon.

It doesn't like to
be in a Poké Ball.

It's known as
the Sky High
Pokémon.

A female Eon
Pokémon.

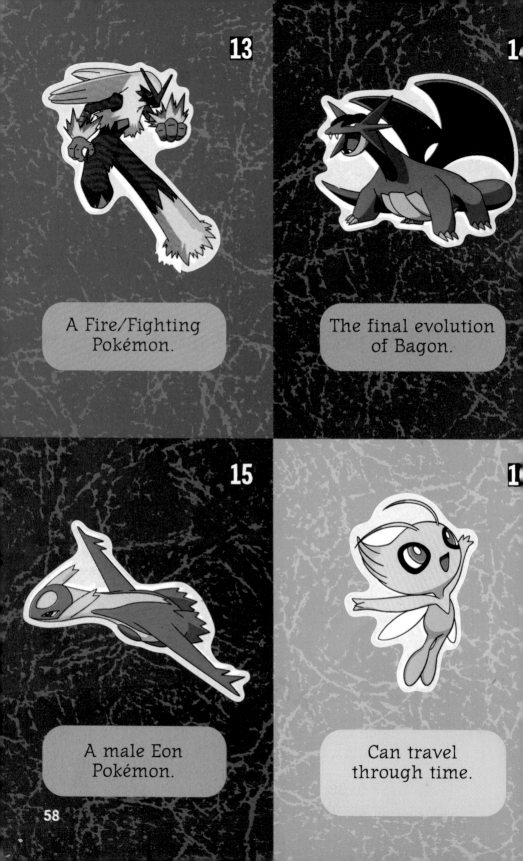

13

A Fire/Fighting
Pokémon.

14

The final evolution
of Bagon.

15

A male Eon
Pokémon.

1

Can travel
through time.

17

Make a wish on
this Pokémon.

18

This legendary
Pokémon lives deep
in the ocean.

19

It deflects attacks
with a pink bubble.

20

The only cloned
Pokémon.

MEMORABLE MOMENTS

Scholastic's pick

Ash and his Pokémon have had some amazing times together over the years. They've laughed, they've cried, and yes, some of them have even fallen in love! This section takes a

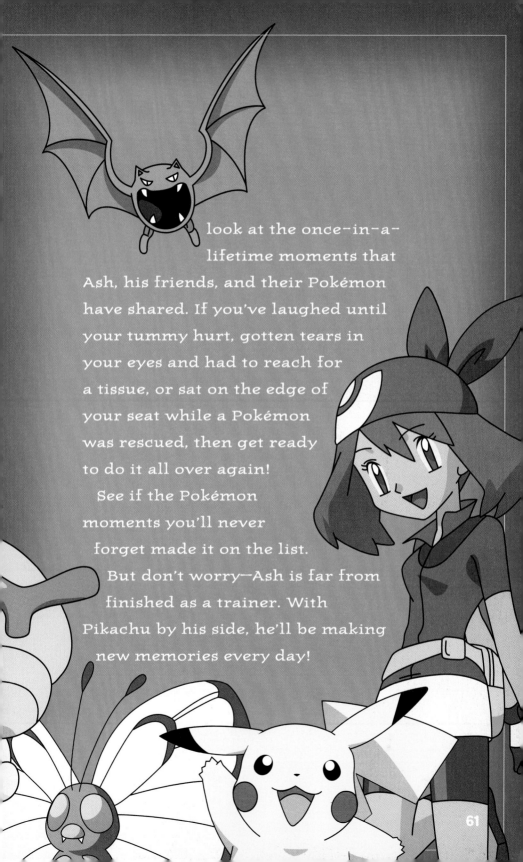

look at the once-in-a-lifetime moments that Ash, his friends, and their Pokémon have shared. If you've laughed until your tummy hurt, gotten tears in your eyes and had to reach for a tissue, or sat on the edge of your seat while a Pokémon was rescued, then get ready to do it all over again!

See if the Pokémon moments you'll never forget made it on the list.

But don't worry—Ash is far from finished as a trainer. With Pikachu by his side, he'll be making new memories every day!

Greatest Pokémon Love Stories

Pokémon and their trainers are always busy battling and training, so how do they ever find the time to fall in love? For some Pokémon, there is always time for romance!

Meowth™ and Meowsy™

Season 2, Episode 217: Hollywood Heartbreak
Before Meowth joined up with Team Rocket, it was a young Pokémon in love. In fact, Meowth was so crazy about another beautiful Meowth that it learned to talk just to impress it. But Meowth's plan backfired. Meowsy thought Meowth was a freak because it could talk. Poor Meowth! He was left brokenhearted.

Butterfree™ and Butterfree™

Season 1, Episode 121: Bye Bye Butterfree
During their mating season, all the Butterfree gather in one spot to fly around and find a mate. Ash, Misty, and Brock hopped into a hot air balloon and let Ash's Butterfree fly. Butterfree fell in love with a pretty pink Butterfree that didn't like Ash's Butterfree at all. But the pink Butterfree had a change of heart when Ash's Butterfree bravely saved all the Butterfree from Team Rocket! Ash let his Butterfree fly off to start a new family.

Totodile™ and Azumarill™ and Totodile™ and Quagsire™

Season 3, Episode 348: Love, Totodile Style
Ash's Totodile is great in battle, but the poor Water Pokémon is always losing its heart! First, Totodile fell in love with Azumarill, a beautiful Water Pokémon. Totodile helped save the Azumarill from Team Rocket, but it didn't matter—the Azumarill was already in love with a Golduck. Totodile was sad, until it met a Quagsire and fell in love again! That didn't work out either, but Totodile bounced back. It takes more than a broken heart to keep this tough little Pokémon down!

Brock™ and—everyone?

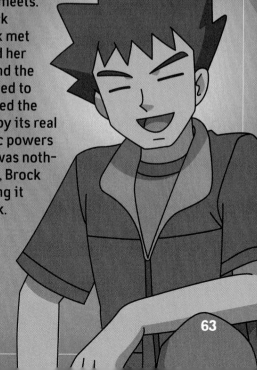

Season 5, Episode 523: Just Waiting On A Friend
Just kidding! Everyone knows that Brock falls in love with every pretty girl he meets. But did you know that once Brock almost got married? When Brock met the beautiful trainer Kimono and her Ninetails, he thought he had found the girl of his dreams. She even agreed to marry him! But Brock soon learned the truth: The Ninetails, abandoned by its real master, used its amazing psychic powers to make Kimono seem real. She was nothing but an illusion! Although sad, Brock helped out the Ninetails by setting it free. But don't worry about Brock. He'll fall in love again—and again and again and again!

Most Dramatic Rescues

If Ash isn't battling in a Pokémon match, he's busy battling Team Rocket or some other bad guys to rescue a Pokémon in distress! Our hero usually wins in the end—but these rescues had us sitting on the edge of our seats!

The Lugia heist

Season 5, Episode 512: A Parent Trapped!

Butch and Cassidy, a team of Pokémon thieves from Team Rocket, stole a baby Lugia. But that was only the first part of their plan. They used the Pokémon as bait in a Lugia trap! When the baby's parent battled desperately to save it, it almost fell right into Butch and Cassidy's clutches. But Ash worked hard at convincing the parent Lugia to trust him—and when it did, Ash and Lugia were able to defeat Butch and Cassidy and rescue the baby Lugia!

Charizard's stuck!

Movie short, Pikachu's Vacation

In *Pikachu's Vacation*, Pikachu and all of its friends were ready to have fun at a special park designed just for Pokémon to play and relax. But their good time came to an end when Charizard got its head stuck in a pipe! It looked like Charizard would stay stuck—until Cubone pitched in and helped all the other Pokémon free Charizard!

Wingull's worry

Season 6, Episode 630: On a Wingull and a Prayer
A sailor named Briney offered to take Ash, May, and Brock to Dewford Island. Along the way, a member of Team Aqua stole Briney's boat and his Wingull, Peeko. Ash and his friends rescued the Water/Flying Pokémon, but the Team Aqua thug got away.

Parent trap!

Feature film, Spell of the Unown
Ash has saved the day more than once, but he never thought he'd have to rescue his own mother! When Entei snatched his mother away before his very eyes, Ash had to save her by battling the mysterious Pokémon, Unown.

Saddest Moments

Sure, Ash and his friends have had a lot of great times together. But there were plenty of times that brought tears to our eyes, too. Better grab a tissue before you start reading!

Pikachu's goodbye

Season 1, Episode 130: Pikacu's Goodbye
When Ash and Pikachu met up with a group of wild Pikachu, Pikachu was the happiest Ash had ever seen it. When it came time to leave, Ash told Pikachu to stay with the other Pokémon. Ash walked away, but at the last minute, Pikachu came running back! Ash may have chosen Pikachu in the beginning, but this time, Pikachu chose Ash!

Charizard finds a new home

Season 3, Episode 329: Charizard's Burning Ambitions
Ash cared for Charizard when it was just a small Charmander abandoned by its master. When Charmander evolved into Charizard, Ash had his strongest Pokémon yet! But all that changed when they visited Charizific Valley. The weakest Charizard there was able to defeat Charizard easily. Charizard was so sad, even Team Rocket felt sorry for it! Ash made the tough decision to leave Charizard there so it could train and get stronger.

Mewtwo strikes back

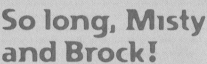

Movie: Mewtwo Strikes Back

In *Mewtwo Strikes Back*, Ash, Misty, and Brock tried to stop Mewtwo from cloning Pokémon and taking over the world! The cloned Pokémon began a huge battle with all the other Pokémon, and it looked like nothing could stop them from fighting. Ash tried to stop the battle and got hurt—and it seemed he might never get up. All of the Pokémon began to cry, and their tears revived Ash.

So long, Misty and Brock!

Season 6, Episode 611: Gotta Catch Ya Later!

Ash, Misty, and Brock have traveled all over together, finding new Pokémon and having adventures. But Misty and Brock both used to be gym leaders. So after the Johto League Silver Conference, Misty and Brock both had to return home to their gyms. The friends were sad to leave each other—and Pokémon fans were sad to see Misty and Brock leave, too!

Happiest Moments

Did that last section depress you? Then read on. Here are some of the happiest moments in Ash's Pokémon journey. It was difficult to just pick a few. After all, just being a Pokémon trainer makes Ash happy!

Caterpie caught!

Season 1, Episode 103: Ash Catches a Pokémon!
At the start of his journey, Ash only had one Pokémon, Pikachu, given to him by Professor Oak. Traveling with Pikachu and Misty through the Virdian Forest, Ash spotted a Caterpie. He threw out a Poké Ball and caught his very first Pokémon!

Ash defeats Gary!

Season 6, Episode 608: Can't Beat The Heat
From the start, Ash and Gary were rivals. Gary always bragged about how he was a better trainer than Ash. And as good as Ash got, he never seemed to be able to compete with Gary. Then came the Johto League Silver Conference. After a fierce battle, Ash's Charizard defeated Gary's Blastoise. The crowd cheered as Ash finally defeated his rival!

Times Team Rocket Almost Succeeded

They try so hard, but Jessie, James, and Meowth never manage to catch Pikachu or get away with one of their crazy schemes. But here are a few times when their plans almost worked. If they can come this close, maybe one day Team Rocket really will win!

Pelipper prevails!

Season 6, Episode 622: You Said A Mouthful

Ash battled a trainer named Anthony and his super strong Pokémon Pelipper, a Water Bird Pokémon. But Ash couldn't win against the Pokémon, which seemed to know every kind of attack: Fire, Grass, Water, even Electric. You name it, and this Pokémon could do it. But how was this possible?

Team Rocket discovered that Anthony was hiding Poké Balls inside of Pelipper's mouth and using the Pokémon inside the balls to deliver the attacks. They threatened to reveal Anthony's secret unless he let them use Pelipper to battle people—with the winner keeping the loser's Pokémon! Before you knew it, Team Rocket had more Pokémon than they could count! But of course, they got too greedy and overstuffed the Pelipper's mouth with Poké Balls. The balls fell out in front of everybody, and Team Rocket had to give all the Pokémon back!

Phantastic Phanpy!

Season 5, Episode 521: Hatching A Plan
Ash was given an egg as a reward by a man and wife who raised Pokémon eggs, and the egg hatched into a Phanpy. But when Phanpy got lost in the woods, Team Rocket managed to convince the cute Ground Pokémon to help them steal Pikachu! They captured Pikachu with Phanpy's help, but Ash won back Phanpy's trust and rescued both it and Pikachu. As usual, Team Rocket went blasting off again.

Catch that Wobbuffet!

Season 4, Episode 435: The Wayward Wobbuffet
On their journey, Ash, Misty, and Brock came across a strange couple with a brand new Poké Ball. The couple asked if they could borrow Pikachu to test out the new ball. Pikachu went inside and was immediately trapped! The strange couple turned out to be none other than Team Rocket in disguise.

Finally, Jessie and James had Pikachu right where they wanted it—trapped inside the ball, it couldn't shock them at all. But there was one problem. The key to the Poké Ball was on a chain around Wobbuffet's neck. With help from Noctowl, Ash got the key from Wobbuffet and rescued Pikachu, too. Team Rocket was really close that time—but not close enough!

Scariest Moments

Let's face it. You've got to be brave to be a Pokémon trainer. You never know what kind of spooky Pokémon you'll meet or creepy new places you'll have to explore. Ash and his friends have had plenty of scares on their journeys. Here are some of their most frightening face-offs ever.

The ghost of Maiden's Peak

Season 1, Episode 120: The Ghost of Maiden's Peak

According to legend, the mysterious mountain known as Maiden's Peak is haunted. As the story goes, a girl waited on top of the peak for her boyfriend to come home, and she was there so long she turned to stone. When Ash and his friends journeyed to Maiden's Peak, Brock and James both fell under the spell of the ghostly girl.

Ash and Misty investigated and found out that a Gastly was behind the haunting! Ash battled the spooky Gastly, who had to leave the peak when the sun rose.

So the ghost of Maiden's Peak is just a legend—or is it? After Ash and his friends left, Gastly returned to Maiden Peak. A ghost girl thanked it for keeping her legend alive. Maiden's Peak really is haunted!

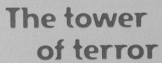

The tower of terror

Season 1, Episode 123: The tower of Terror

When Ash needed to catch a Ghost Pokémon, he had to go to a spooky old tower that was said to be haunted. Ash, Misty, and Brock went to the tower in the middle of the night. Once inside, they were met by the terrifying sight of Gastly, Haunter, and Gengar. Brock and Misty ran in terror, leaving Ash and Pikachu all by themselves. Ash overcame his fear and made friends with the ghosts, even leaving his body for a little bit and experiencing what life is like as a Ghost Pokémon.

Fossil fear

Season 1, Episode 146: Attack of the Prehistoric Pokémon

Ash, Misty, and Brock passed through Grandpa Canyon and got the scare of their lives! People were digging for prehistoric Pokémon fossils, and when Team Rocket lit some dynamite to do some digging of their own, Ash and his friends got trapped in an underground cave. Strange, glowing eyes stared at them in the darkness. They were surrounded by fossil Pokémon! Kabuto, Kabutops, Omanyte, and Omastar started to attack. An Aerodactyl almost ate Ash before Charizard rescued him.

Spooky Sabrina

Season 1, Episode 124: Haunter versus Kadabra

Ash faced the spookiest trainer ever when he took on Sabrina, who had unbelievable psychic power and even more powerful Psychic Pokémon. This time Ash had to battle not only for a badge but also to rescue Misty and Brock! Sabrina had changed them into dolls and locked them in her dollhouse. Ash used his Haunter, which saved the day by making Sabrina laugh and breaking the eerie spell over her. Misty and Brock were freed!

Most Amazing Evolutions

Evolution! Every Pokémon trainer wants their Pokémon to evolve into stronger and smarter creatures. Every evolution is amazing—but these are some that are hard to forget.

Charmeleon to Charizard

Season 1, Episode 146: Attack of the Prehistoric Pokémon

When Ash, Misty, and Brock met up with some ancient Aerodactyl, Ash almost became Pokémon chow! An Aerodactyl swooped up Ash and flew away with him. Charmeleon wanted to save its master but wasn't strong enough to fight the Flying Pokémon. So the tough little Charmeleon evolved into Charizard, chased after the Aerodactyl, and saved Ash!

Zubat to Goldbat

Season 4, Episode 408: Hassle in the Castle

Team Rocket was at it again—causing trouble for Ash and his friends! While the gang was visiting a castle, Team Rocket managed to trap themselves and Brock in the castle's basement, which also happened to be a maze! They finally found their way out, and then Team Rocket snatched Brock's Zubat. But Zubat evolved into Goldbat and sent Team Rocket blasting off with a super powerful supersonic attack!

Metapod to Butterfree

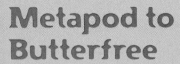

Season 1, Episode 104: Challenge of the Samurai
After Ash caught his first Pokémon, Caterpie, it soon evolved into Metapod. But Ash didn't know how long it would take for Metapod to evolve into Butterfree. Ash was in for a surprise when Metapod threw itself in front of an attacking Beedrill to protect Ash from its stinger. The stinger tore open Metapod's shell, and Metapod was transformed into the beautiful Butterfree—while saving Ash's life!

Togepi to Togetic

Season 7, Togepi's Paradise
When Misty and the gang were cornered by General Hanzou and Team Rocket, Togepi proved that little Pokémon are tough, too. It transported them to another dimension populated entirely by Togepis. When General Hanzou and Team Rocket came to make trouble, Togepi fought them off by doing the amazing—evolving into Togetic!

Pokémon in Peril

Pokémon can get injured in battle or sick with an illness. Luckily, Nurse Joy is always ready to help at the nearest Pokémon Center. But sometimes it's a matter of life and death to find a Pokémon the help it needs.

Meowth and the Blinking Coin

Season 1, Episode 144: The Problem with Paras

For once, Team Rocket had other things on its mind than just stealing Pokémon. Meowth, their talking Pokémon, became very sick. The coin on the middle of his forehead started blinking, letting Jessie and James know that Meowth needed help. They rushed him to a woman who makes healing potions for Pokémon, and Meowth was cured!

The care of the Corphish

Season 6, Episode 636: A Corphish Out of Water

After Ash's newest Pokémon, Corphish, was injured during a battle with Team Rocket, Ash had to rush it to the nearest Pokémon center. Unfortunately, a school of hungry Carvanha surrounded the center. But Ash, with some help from May, managed to defeat the Carvanha and get Corphish the treatment it needed.

Sparkle is sick!

Season 4, Episode 451: Fight For The Light!
Ash, Misty, and Brock met a trainer named Jasmine who had a very sick Ampharos named Sparkle. The medicine needed to cure it was all the way in Cianwood City, so Ash and his friends offered to get the medicine. The journey wasn't easy, but they got back in time to save Sparkle!

Trapped!

Season 4, Episode 410: A Hot Water Battle
Attacked by Aipom and lost in the woods, it looked like things couldn't get any worse for Chikorita, Cyndaquil, and Totodile. But when they fell into a hidden cave in the forest floor, things got much worse. Then Meowth got stuck, too. Luckily, the Pokémon learned to work together, and they all found their way home.

Team Rocket's Worst Attempts Ever at Stealing Pikachu

Poor Team Rocket! They've tried and tried to steal Ash's Pikachu but have never been able to pull it off. It almost makes you feel sorry for them. They always fail, but sometimes their attempts to steal Pikachu ends up as such a disaster that it just has to go into the Hall of Fame.

Pikachu or Pikachild?

Season 2, Episode 202: The Purr-fect Hero

When Ash visited a school and talked to the children about being Pokémon trainers, Team Rocket showed up disguised as magicians. They grabbed Pikachu, put it into a box, and abracadabra! Pikachu disappeared and Meowth popped up in its place. Team Rocket left, thinking they had finally captured Pikachu. But when they opened the box, they found one of the schoolchildren inside! Ash rescued the boy—with a little help from Meowth!

Meowth and Pikachu team up

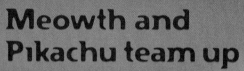

Season 6, Episode 612: Hoenn Alone!
When would Meowth and Pikachu ever team up to help each other? When Team Rocket put them both in danger! Team Rocket snatched Pikachu off a ship that Ash and Pikachu were traveling on. They escaped with Pikachu at the nearest port but ended up losing both Meowth and Pikachu in a scary neighborhood. Meowth and Pikachu worked together to fight off a gang of spooky Haunters. Ash and Officer Jenny arrived to save Pikachu, but Team Rocket got away once again.

The awful Arbotank

Season 3, Episode 320: Tanks A Lot!
Jessie, James, and Meowth sank all of their money into their latest weapon, the Arbotank. This powerful tank could move over any terrain—the perfect method for chasing Ash and Pikachu! Before Team Rocket could even try to nab the Electric Pokémon, Togepi and Sentret hijacked the tank and went on a wild joyride. Ash, Misty, and Brock eventually caught up to the tank and got Togepi and Sentret out. Then Pikachu blasted the tank with an Electric attack, leaving Team Rocket without their weapon—and once again without Pikachu!

Answer key:

pages 24-33

WHO'S THAT
POKéMON? (part 1)

1. WINGULL
2. METAGROSS
3. PELIPPER
4. BLAZIKEN
5. WAILORD
6. TAILLOW
7. BELLOSSOM
8. SUNKERN
9. HO-OH
10. LUGIA
11. MEOWTH
12. PHANPY
13. ENTEI
14. SLOWKING
15. WOBBUFFET
16. ROSELIA
17. MAKUHITA
18. TOTODILE
19. MEWTWO
20. HAUNTER
21. SLOWPOKE
22. ALAKAZAM
23. UNOWN
24. RAIKOU
25. PSYDUCK
26. ARTICUNO
27. KYOGRE
28. MUDKIP
29. TREECKO
30. JIGGLYPUFF
31. BUTTERFREE
32. NATU
33. PIKACHU
34. SUICUNE
35. QUAGSIRE
36. JIRACHI
37. SWAMPERT
38. ABSOL
39. SKITTY
40. CLAYDOL

pages 54-59

WHO'S THAT
POKéMON? (part 2)

1. TREECKO
2. TORCHIC
3. MUDKIP
4. ABSOL
5. KYOGRE
6. SCEPTILE
7. SWAMPERT
8. GROUDON
9. CHARIZARD
10. PIKACHU
11. RAYQUAZA
12. LATIAS
13. BLAZIKEN
14. SALAMENCE
15. LATIOS
16. CELEBI
17. JIRACHI
18. LUGIA
19. MEW
20. MEWTWO

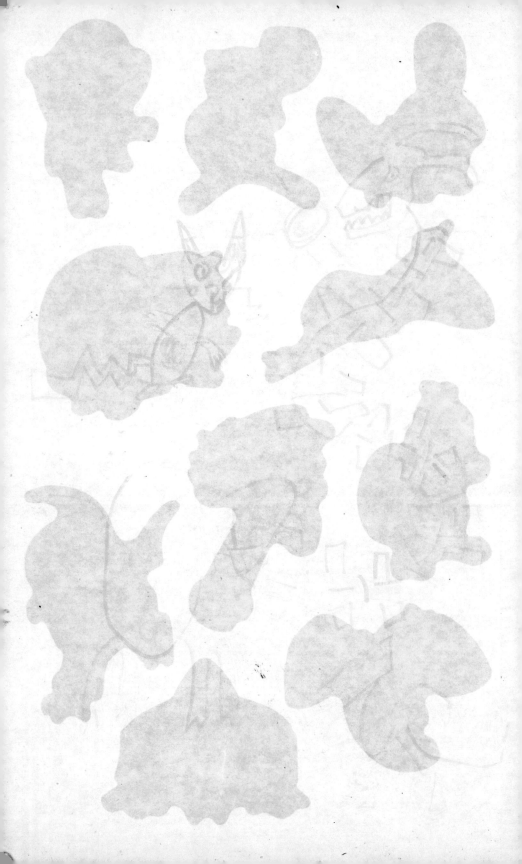